Born to Run

The Story of Brittany Young

By
Barbara Rudow

www.scobre.com

Photography by Patty Holbrook
Edited by Helen Glenn Court
Cover Art & Layout by Michael Lynch

TOUCHDOWN EDITION
This story is based on the real life of Brittany Young, although some names, quotes, and details of events have been altered.

For Taylor and Allison.

Chapter One

The Burn Pit

Brittany Young is as unique as the Hawaiian Islands that she calls home. Brittany is a fun-loving, sixteen-year-old girl growing up on the beautiful island of Maui, which is the seventh of the eight major Hawaiian islands. Although Maui is small enough to drive around in less than a day, there are more than 100,000 residents and Brittany considers herself lucky to be one of them.

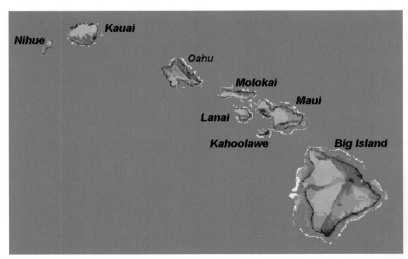

This lively teenager enjoys all the special things that Maui has to offer. She loves to surf, snorkel, paddle, and barbeque at the beach and to enjoy world-famous sunsets with her family and friends. Brittany's college plans will likely take her to the continental United States, 2,500 miles from her island home, but the spirit of the islands will always be with her.

When you meet Brittany, you are instantly greeted with a cheerful, easy smile that makes you think her life is as carefree as the tropical birds that sing her awake each morning. But Brittany's life has been anything but carefree. When Brittany was only seven years old, her world was shattered, and her life changed forever. . .

The date was May 24, 1997. It seemed like a normal spring day. Seven-year-old Brittany was returning from a birthday party. As the Young family car turned the corner onto Cooke Road, Brittany and her brother Jake made their usual request. They begged their mom to let them out of the car so they could walk the rest of the way home. The Youngs lived along a mile-long dusty road, dotted with houses, each hidden behind a mask of eucalyptus trees.

Brittany and her brother Jake stand in their front yard.

Mrs. Young pulled over, and Jake was out of the car in an instant. Brittany, as usual, was flying right behind him. Jake was nine years old, eighteen months older than his sister. The two seemed attached at the hip.

When Mrs. Young called out to Brittany, reminding her to put her shoes on, Brittany resisted. "Jake doesn't have shoes on," she said.

Before Mrs. Young could argue, the two children were off and running up the road barefoot. Their laughter bounced off the trees as they passed an old protea farm. In its day, this particular farm was beautiful—it looked like a glorious burst of fireworks! Protea are one of the world's most unusual flowers. Native to South Africa, they grow especially well in the Kula area of Upcountry Maui. Kula, where Brittany lived, is a residential area sitting on the side of Haleakala, which is a dormant volcano.

A Protea flower in full blossom.

3

Jake stopped when they reached the old farm and so did Brittany. The owner had let most of the flowers die off a while ago. He had neglected many things on his land. In fact, a grand old eucalyptus tree used to stand on the edge of his property. The awesome tree towered over the road. It had been removed a few years earlier, but the giant stump had stubbornly remained. The owner did not want to pay to have the stump taken out, so he decided to burn it. He burned cuttings and trash in the center of the stump—turning it into a dangerous fire pit.

When the stump finally sank into the earth, it left behind a crater fourteen feet across and more than five feet deep. Jake stared at the hole where the stump had once sat bravely grasping the ground with its massive roots. He then crept closer to the crater, with Brittany close behind him. When they got to the edge, they peered in. The kids had watched the tree shrink in size for many months, but never quite believed that it would really be gone.

In the past, they had seen open flames in the stump. The fire had scared them away from peering this closely. Today, though, the white ash looked like a blanket of snow covering the hole. Jake poked his stick into the circle. The fire appeared to be gone. What they didn't understand was that although there were no flames, the coals were still burning hot underneath the white cover.

Jake and Brittany circled the crater, poking their sticks into the ash. Brittany reminded Jake that they were supposed to go right home. Jake assured her that they'd go in a minute. With those words still hanging in the air, he stepped onto the inside ledge that lined the pit. It was like taking the first step into a pool. Even though she was anxious about getting home on time, Brittany followed him. Jake had made it to the other side of the crater, so Brittany assumed that the ground was solid everywhere—but it wasn't.

When Brittany put her left foot down onto the ledge, she began to sink. At first she didn't realize what was going on. It happened so quickly. Before she knew it, she had sunk up to her knees. It was then that Brittany began to feel intense heat beneath her feet, and a bitter acid taste in her mouth. There was a moment of stunned silence, when even the birds seemed to hold their breath. That silence was immediately shattered by an endless, piercing scream.

Brittany's legs were encased in hot coals that had been burning for the past three days. The temperature was around 1200 degrees, quickly destroying Brittany's thin legs as she struggled to escape. Unable to use her legs, Brittany hoisted herself out of the hole with her arms. At this point, she wasn't fully aware of what she was doing. All she could think about was getting home. She could feel her shins burning. Her feet were burning, too.

Then, something amazing happened. With her legs burned so badly that it would take months before she would be able to walk again, Brittany started to run. Defying logic, and science, she shot up from the burning hole in the ground and sprinted up the road, skin falling off her legs with every step she took. Her long, beautiful strides defied her burning legs—and defied the fact that a person burned this badly, should not have been able to move, let alone run.

Brittany will always remember looking down at her feet and seeing what she describes as "transparent toenails floating in blood" Then, looking below her knees, she saw where black rings had formed with puss oozing from her raw, discolored skin. These were the scariest moments of her life.

By the time she reached the house, Brittany's feet had swollen to four times their normal size. The burns made her legs unrecognizable. Her remarkable survival instinct had propelled her forward—which is the only way to explain her running through the terrible pain.

Brittany's father was outside mowing the lawn with ear muffs on. He was stopped cold by a heart-wrenching scream that his ear muffs couldn't block out. He turned off the mower and ran to his daughter. Seeing the damage to her legs, he lifted Brittany and hurried toward the house, yelling for her mom.

Mrs. Young heard the screams too. As she got to the door she saw her husband running toward her, Brittany in his arms. Just then, Jake came running up the road, tears streaming down his cheeks. He was unable to speak, likely in a state of shock. This was his baby sister whom he adored and protected. One minute she was across the crater from him, and the next she had bolted up the hill, screaming. He didn't even know what had happened.

Mrs. Young fought back tears as she hurriedly placed Brittany in the back seat of the car. Then, she remembered her first aid training. She knew that she was not supposed to put ice directly on the burns, but that she had to cool them down. She quickly ran towels under cold water and wrapped each of Brittany's legs, trying to block out the screams. This needed to be done, even though it hurt.

In most places, the immediate thing to do would be to call 911. But the Young home, located on a very secluded section of Haleakala, was difficult to get to, and it would take a long time for an ambulance to make the trip. They decided to drive the thirty minutes down the mountain and head to the hospital themselves.

This photo of Haleakala shows why getting an ambulance to Brittany's home was so difficult.

Brittany sat with her towel-wrapped feet dangling in a cooler of ice. Mr. Young drove, trying to go fast, but also dodging bumps and potholes that came with unpaved roads and rural living. The drive down the sugarcane-lined mountain, which was usually so peaceful, seemed like an eternal nightmare.

Luckily, the emergency room at Maui Memorial Hospital wasn't crowded. When Brittany came in, she was treated immediately. The doctor on call, however, was not experienced with burns. It took the help of a seasoned nurse to recognize that Brittany's injuries were severe and would need more extensive care than Maui Memorial could offer. This special nurse also gave Brittany a teddy bear. Brittany says that the bear was a source of strength for her. She named him Boo Boo, and has him to this day.

After attempting to treat the wounds, the medical team decided to have Brittany flown to the island of Oahu immediately.

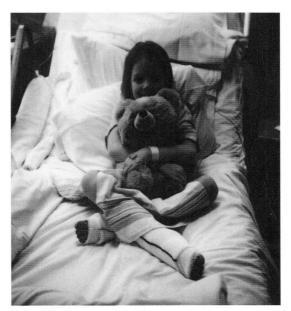

Brittany, in her hospital bed with her teddy bear Boo Boo.

Honolulu, which is the largest city on Oahu, has several specialized hospitals—including a burn center. Maui doesn't have a burn center and without proper care, Brittany's prognosis would not be good. As the doctors wheeled her stretcher onto the two-prop plane, they knew they had to hurry. Every minute would help save Brittany's legs, giving her the chance to walk again.

Besides Brittany and the paramedics, only one person could fit into the plane. This was devastating, because neither parent wanted to leave Brittany's side. They decided that Mrs. Young would accompany Brittany on the twenty-five minute flight to Oahu. The flight seemed to take about ten times that long.

As the plane soared above the clouds, Brittany lay on the stretcher, her small frame dwarfed by the blankets and straps that held her still. She was in great pain, and the noisy plane was so loud she could barely talk. Mrs. Young stared out the window and tried not to panic. Who could have imagined that instead of going to the beach for a Memorial Day picnic, they would be flying to a hospital in Oahu? Her beautiful daughter, who should have been home dancing in the waves, was now lying on a gurney, wracked with pain.

These thoughts were interrupted when the pilot announced that they were five minutes from landing. Mrs. Young tried to give her daughter a reassuring smile but Brittany saw the fear in her mother's eyes. Brittany squeezed her hand and forced a smile. She was being strong and brave, but the worst was far from over.

Chapter Two

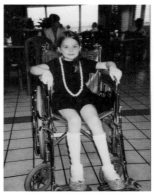

The Road to Recovery

The doctors had bad and good news for Brittany. The bad news was that fifteen percent of her body had been burned. In many spots, the burns were third degree—which was quite serious. Her feet were the worst. The doctors were actually afraid that she would lose several toes on her left foot.

The good news was that it was a "clean burn." As it turned out, it was lucky that Brittany hadn't been wearing shoes that day. If she had been, they would have melted into her feet. In that case, the prognosis would have been much worse. The doctors probably would have had to amputate.

Dr. Linda Rosen, an ER physician, handled Brittany's case. She was a great doctor. Unfortunately, she wasn't a magician and she couldn't make the pain disappear. Dr. Rosen explained that when people are badly burned, it feels like the injured area is still burning, even for several days. Only time would heal Brittany's wounds.

Brittany's father made his way out to Oahu the following morning. She was happy to see him. Although her brother had stayed behind, Brittany talked to Jake on the phone from the hospital. Brittany also missed her little sister. But three-year-old Makenna wasn't much for phone conversation and didn't understand that Brittany was badly hurt and not coming home any time soon.

The Young family, standing in front of their home in Kula.

As the days passed by, Brittany really started to miss her friends at school. Her classmates had sent so many presents, cards, and balloons that her hospital room looked like a party supply store.

The cards and phone calls from friends and family were great, but living in a hospital was no fun. After a month had passed and she was still there, she began to get very impatient. Her body was slowly healing, but she still had to endure many hours of painful procedures and physical therapy. After all, she could neither stand nor walk.

Three weeks after her accident, the fact that her legs were still immobile made her sprint up the hill on Cooke Road—when her legs were on fire—twice as amazing. In fact, when Mrs. Young told the story to Brittany's doctors, they were all left scratching their heads. It didn't make sense that the little girl would have been able to move like that in the condition her legs were in. What the doctors didn't know was that this girl was special—she was born to run.

As special as Brittany was, her legs were still in serious condition. One of the main issues she faced every day was infection. Burn victims are especially susceptible to infections because their skin, which protects them, is gone. To fight this, Brittany's bandages were changed two times each day. Unfortunately, this procedure was the most painful thing she had to endure during her hospital stay. Twice every day Brittany would be taken to a sound-proof room with giant surgical sinks.

Once there, they would take off her bandages and submerse her legs in warm water. Then they had to scrub them with gauze for twenty minutes to remove all the old skin. While they scrubbed, Brittany clenched a Popsicle stick wrapped in tape between her teeth to keep from screaming. The pain was so unbearable that Brittany bit through it every time.

Brittany later described this procedure. "Imagine taking sand paper to a deep cut," she said, "to the muscle or even bone, and rubbing back and forth to try to remove layers of skin. Now, imagine that all over your feet and shins."

Brittany welcomed any escape from the pain and was thrilled when just such a distraction came in the form of a visitor. For the first three weeks of her hospital stay, Brittany had been stuck in her room. By the fourth week, though, the pain had subsided enough for her to sit in a wheelchair and move around a bit. One of her favorite places to go was the playroom. Her activities were limited, but she was able to play board games, do arts and crafts, build puzzles, and play cards.

On this special day, though, Brittany was too excited to play. The children were told that Miss Universe 1997 would be coming to visit them! Brittany recalls being mesmerized when Miss Universe, Brook Mahealani Lee, walked into the room. She was wearing a massive, diamond-studded tiara, which Brittany later got to wear. Miss Lee was from Hawaii and had come to the hospital to cheer up the young patients. She played cards with Brittany and told her all about her travels. Brittany says that her visit was the highlight of her hospital stay.

Wearing her diamond-studded tiara, Brittany sits with Miss Universe 1997, Brook Mahealani Lee.

Although the visit was awesome, what Brittany really wanted was to be outside playing with Jake, Makenna, and her friends. She was tired of bandage changes and physical therapy. But she knew that although her treatments were very painful, they were also very necessary. Physical therapy had to be done before she could go home from the hospital, so she gave it everything she had. She went every day for an hour and refused to cry.

One thing that Brittany enjoyed, which she could never do at home, was to eat anything she wanted. That's right—anything! Burn victims lose a lot of weight because their body uses about 10,000 to 15,000 calories a day just to fight the burn. This means that burn victims need to take in a lot of calories to maintain their weight. To put this into perspective, a normal diet suggests that a person eats about 2,000 calories per day. Brittany's doctors wanted her to eat at least five times this amount! Brittany recalls this as the only time in her life when she was able to eat all the candy she wanted. She lived on Rolos. The doctors didn't care what she ate as long as she ate a lot of calories, even from junk food.

In fact, Dr. Rosen walked into Brittany's room some days with cans of whipped cream, asking her to eat all of it! Despite their best efforts, Brittany still lost ten pounds during her hospital stay, which was too much for her small body.

Despite losing weight, Brittany could tell that she was getting better. Still, she had been in the hospital for more than a month and was starting to doubt whether she'd ever see home again. Finally, in late June, six full weeks after she was airlifted to Oahu, Brittany was wheeled out of the sliding doors for the last time. It was a sunny day and the tropical air was like a taste of heaven. She was finally free!

As she left the hospital, she took a final look around the playroom. She observed the kids around her closely. Although she had been living with them for over a month, she never really thought about what they were forced to endure. Naturally, she had focused on her own pain.

Now, with the worst of it behind her, she looked at the other patients with great compassion. She wanted to make them all better—and take them all home with her. She noticed that many of them had no hair because of chemotherapy treatments, and that some were so deformed that she couldn't even guess what had caused it. Tears welled up in her eyes. Even at seven years old, sitting in a wheelchair with burned legs and feet, Brittany knew that she was lucky.

Brittany was forever changed when she left the hospital. Sure, she was excited to get back to her old life. But even as a young girl, she knew that nothing would ever be the same. Especially not the way she looked at the world. She left that day with bandaged legs, and an inner strength that most people never achieve.

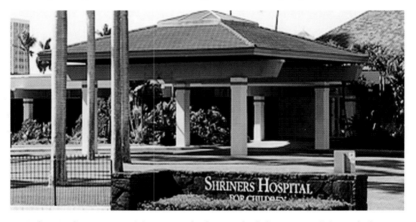

The Shriners Hospital for Children in Honolulu.

Chapter Three

Back in Maui

When Brittany returned to her home on Maui, she couldn't stop smiling. But being home didn't mean that her ordeal was over. Sure, she was able to walk on her own, but she had to move very slowly. Her feet had healed enough to step on them, but the skin on her legs was paper thin. Any contact—even the slightest bump— would cause the skin to fall off. This happened a week after her homecoming, and was extremely painful.

The doctors let Brittany know that she wouldn't be able to wear shoes for another four months. Her mom, though, found a pair of oversized, soft-top sandals that Brittany was able to use when she went outside. The sandals were funky, striped, and kind of cool. Because the tops of Brittany's feet were the most tender, she had to take extra care of them. Before she put the sandals on, she put on a thick sock over her Jobst stockings to protect her feet.

Jobst stockings are medical stockings that helped protect Brittany's legs. She had to wear them for two full years after her accident, changing them every month. They are super tight, compression stockings that increase blood flow and reduce swelling. These stocking were a constant reminder to Brittany—and everyone around her—of her accident.

Her activities were extremely limited but doctors did give her permission to swim. Brittany loved the water, so this meant the world to her. The public pool in Pukalani, the neighboring town only ten minutes from her house, was her favorite place. Before her injury, she met her friends there almost every day. It had been two months since she had stepped into the burn pit and she hadn't been out of the house much since she returned from the hospital two weeks earlier. She was anxious after all this time to hang out with her friends Hannah and Claire.

The public pool in Pukalani.

In the locker room, Brittany changed into her bathing suit. As she and Hannah made their way to the pool, she gripped Hannah's arm to prevent falling. They were about to step into the water when the lifeguard blew his whistle loudly. Then, in front of everyone, he told Brittany that she couldn't swim with her stockings on. It was against the rules. She quietly tried to explain to him that she couldn't take them off, but he wouldn't listen. Despite the desperation in her voice, he refused to let Brittany in the water.

Brittany was crushed and totally embarrassed. She headed back to the locker room, where she sat alone while her friends swam. That was the first time Brittany realized that she was different. She was beginning to see that not everyone was going to be understanding or sympathetic. In fact, people could be cruel.

A few months later, with that incident in the rearview mirror, Brittany began third grade. At this point, she was able to walk fairly normally. She still attended physical therapy once a week, and had to go The Shriners Hospitals for Children on Oahu to be examined and fitted for new Jobst stockings every few months. Although she still couldn't do anything too active, like running, Brittany tried not to dwell on it. For now, she was just happy to be walking. Of course, when she closed her eyes at night, she would dream of sprinting down the road, or on the beach—her legs working the way they once had.

Overall, Brittany was proud of the progress she had made. In fact, when her teacher asked her to tell the class about her accident, she was happy to. Standing in front of twenty-five students, she began by telling them about the fire pit and her burns. That seemed to make the kids uncomfortable, so she shifted gears and focused on fun things like eating lots of candy, staying up late, and meeting Miss Universe.

When asked what the best part was, Brittany told them about the "recovery" cruise she went on over the summer. Brittany's grandparents thought the family needed a break from hospital and physical therapy sessions, so they took the entire family on a cruise around the Hawaiian Islands. Of course, Brittany was limited by her injuries and wasn't able to fully participate in all the activities.

Her family got the chance to hike Kilauea, which is an active volcano on Hawaii (The Big Island). Kilauea had recently erupted, so they were able to see lava actually flowing down the mountain into the ocean. It was awesome! Although Brittany wasn't able to walk on the rocky ground because of her sensitive legs, her mother had carried her on her back so that she could see everything up close.

Mount Kilauea . . . erupting!

When her classmates asked Brittany what the worst part of her ordeal was, she didn't hesitate in making a joke. She told them how mad she was when the doctors cut off her favorite shorts when she got to the hospital. After everyone stopped laughing, a boy in the class asked if he could see her legs.

At this question, Brittany hesitated. She was definitely proud of the progress she had made in her recovery. But she also knew that there was scarring, especially on her left foot—the first foot to slip into the pit. To fix this, doctors had suggested grafting. Grafting is a surgical procedure that transplants living tissue to replace other, damaged tissue. For Brittany, this would have meant taking skin from her buttocks and moving it to her feet. It would have been very painful and would have left a scar on her buttocks. If one little thing went wrong during the procedure, which it sometimes did, they would have to start all over again. After a great deal of thought, she and her parents decided against it.

She thought about this decision while the class leaned in closer to check out her legs, as Brittany slowly unwrapped the bandages. Once exposed, most of the kids stared at Brittany's feet and legs sympathetically.

The boy who had asked to see it, however, right away yelled out, "Ugh, that's gross!"

Brittany was devastated and quickly covered up her legs. She had not considered how her legs would look to others. To her, the scarring was no big deal. After all, she remembered the kids at The Shriners Hospital and all of their serious burns and illnesses. Compared to theirs, her scars were minor. It had never occurred to her that her classmates would look at her injuries and be grossed out. Brittany felt ashamed, which made her uncomfortable and sad. It also made her more determined than ever to get better.

She worked extra hard on her therapy, hoping that she would be "normal" again someday soon. She followed doctor's orders and didn't try to do the active things she wasn't supposed to do, even though it was tempting. At recess, when her friends and classmates were playing tag or soccer, Brittany read a book or hung out with her friend Zoe. The thing she needed most was time. The skin needed to heal, and as frustrating as that was, there was nothing she could do to speed it up.

Two years later, by fifth grade, Brittany considered herself completely healed. She still had to go to the hospital in Oahu two times each year so that they could monitor her progress, but her therapy was now complete. The doctors told her that she no longer needed to wear the hot, itchy Jobst stockings. This thrilled her, of course! So did the next piece of news. After two years of recovery, she was given the go-ahead to play whatever sports she wanted.

After getting cleared by her doctors, Brittany spent a lot of time swimming, snorkeling and boogie-boarding in the sparkling, aquamarine water of Maui's beaches. Another activity she jumped back into was hiking.

On Maui, many hiking trails lead to beautiful waterfalls like this one.

The event that marked Brittany's first real athletic experience, though, was the Kula Elementary School's Annual Fun Run. This school fundraiser was a big event in which students raced twice around the playing fields at their school. Brittany had not run it since the first grade, so she was very excited about the race.

By race time, she was bouncing with excited energy. Still, she didn't have any expectations of winning. She was just glad to be participating. When the whistle blew, Brittany exploded out front. As she ran, it was as if her legs were talking to her. They were telling her how happy they were to be moving again—they were anxious to share with Brittany just how fast they could carry her. She wasn't even breathing hard as she finished her first lap with a huge smile on her face. She felt strong as her unbandaged legs pumped hard through each stride. With all the physical therapy she had gone through, her legs, though covered by delicate skin, were tremendously powerful.

Running was the most amazing feeling in the world! Her ponytail whipped back as she sprinted, and the rush of adrenaline that pumped through her body was awesome. As she made her way around the fields during the second and final lap, she honestly didn't want the run to end. If nobody was around, she would have happily run a third lap.

Brittany was only about a hundred yards away from the finish line when she realized that her friend Lindsay was just a few strides behind her. The rest of the kids were quite a bit farther back. Lindsay had won this event for the past few years and everyone assumed that she would win it again. Brittany knew that winning would mean a lot to Lindsay—even more than it meant to Brittany. Nobody, including Lindsay, expected Lindsay to be beaten. And especially not by a girl who only a short while ago was not even able to walk!

Brittany was easily in first place when she slowed down and waited for her friend to catch up. When the two girls crossed the finish line together, it was a great feeling. For Brittany, this race wasn't about finishing first. In her eyes, she had won the race the moment she started to run it.

Chapter Four

Who's Got Spirit?

The following fall, Brittany jumped into her middle school years with unbridled enthusiasm. She still had to go to the hospital in Oahu for checkups twice during the year, but she was having no pain in her legs or feet. The scarring was going to be permanent, but Brittany had accepted that. She was happy to be back wearing her slippers (flip-flops is what you call them if you're not from Hawaii) and it didn't bother her that her feet showed. If she ever had a moment of regret about her appearance, she reminded herself of some of the other children she'd met—the ones who would never walk, let alone run, again.

When Brittany was twelve years old, she celebrated her recovery by learning the sport of the ancient Hawaiians —surfing. Maui boasts some of the best surf spots in the world but Brittany, because of her burns, had never been able to experience them. She was so excited to finally be healed enough to surf that she spent nearly every weekend at Puamana Park or Launiupoko, two popular surf spots on the west side of Maui.

Brittany and her father standing beside her new surf board.

Brittany immediately fell in love with the sport. She loved the challenge of catching a wave on her longboard, and the thrill she got when she become one with the wave. She also loved the peaceful side of surfing. Sometimes she would sit quietly on her board waiting for the next set of waves, watching green sea turtles swim nearby. In the winter, she would look out and see the humpback whales that are regular visitors to the waters off Maui.

The humpback whales faithfully travel every year from their feeding grounds in the Arctic Ocean near Alaska, all the way to

Hawaii in the Pacific Ocean. When most people on the mainland are looking for the first snow of the winter, the Mauians are looking for the first whale, which usually arrives in mid-November. They are always spectacular to see, whether you are a first-time visitor, or an appreciative islander like Brittany.

Most of Brittany's other activities now centered on her school, Seabury Hall. This independent college preparatory school for grades six through twelve, sits one mile above Makawao Town. Makawao means "forest beginning," an apt name for this beautiful town. Makawao is known for the magnificent jacaranda trees whose lavender blooms paint a colorful contrast with the deep blue sky. Seabury Hall sits on fifty-six acres nestled amidst a spectacular mesh of rolling pasture and dense forest. Peeking down on Maui's North Shore and the West Maui Mountains, Seabury Hall is afforded an amazing backdrop of expansive blue ocean.

Brittany balanced her studies with lots of extracurricular activities. She starred in school plays (she was an elf in *The Hobbit* and a pirate in *Treasure Island*), played various sports, and served on school committees. Brittany loved it all, but her favorite activity in middle school was being part of the spirit committee.

The spirit committee is responsible for getting students involved and enthusiastic about school activities while generating school spirit. Brittany's favorite event was Spirit Week. The committee picks a different theme for each day of the week and all the students dress accordingly. There are crazy hair days, superhero days, 1970s days, and even pirate days.

Another one of Brittany's favorites is the Winterim program. Brittany recalls her eighth-grade Winterim as a memorable experience that forever etched the beauty of Maui in her heart.

Winterim is a four-day excursion outside of the classroom for students to explore various areas of interest.

The Winterim course that Brittany chose was a hike into the Haleakala Crater. Brittany is very interested in the study of nature so this was an exciting opportunity for her. It only takes about an hour to drive from Brittany's home up through the clouds to the top of Haleakala. Hiking down into the crater itself, however, takes considerably longer because the crater is very steep and the hiking is strenuous. Brittany's legs and feet were now strong enough to make this multiday trip. There are very few people in the world who have hiked into the crater of a volcano. Brittany is one of them.

Brittany, center, during her Winterim adventure into Haleakala Crater.

Haleakala, which means "house of the sun," is a dormant volcano that last erupted in 1790. It is 10,000 feet high and has a crater 3,000 feet deep and 21 miles in circumference—which is large enough to hold the entire island of Manhattan! The Seabury Winterim group spent three nights at rustic cabins spread out within the crater. They saw native plants, such as the Haleakala Silversword (Ahinahina), which is part of the sunflower family. Haleakala is actually the only place on the planet where this unique flower is found. The Haleakala Silversword is unique because it has a lifespan of five to twenty years, and during that entire time it only blooms once. After that, it dies.

Haleakala Silversword in full bloom.

Brittany had a great time hiking and learning about Haleakala, but it was the quiet time that she loved most. One night a few of the kids decided to sleep outside, even though the temperature can drop below freezing. Brittany was a member of this adventurous group. As she was lying in her sleeping bag, trying to stay warm, Brittany enjoyed herself stargazing under the watchful eye of a perfect crescent moon. She woke with frost on her sleeping bag and the peaceful beauty of the morning enveloped her. In these moments, she fully appreciated the expression that is known to those who live on Maui: "Maui No Ka Oi," which means "Maui is the best."

Brittany and her friends, Jazzy and Erin, return to Haleakala Crater a few years later. They huddle up to stay warm just after sunrise.

The Seabury sports clubs also played a major role in Brittany's life during middle school. Brittany had fallen behind athletically because of her years of inactivity. This didn't discourage her, however. It just made her focus twice as hard on catching up.

The middle school sports schedule is divided into quarters, allowing Brittany to do cross country, volleyball, basketball, and track. Brittany enjoyed all of these sports, but the two running clubs quickly moved to the forefront of her mind and heart. They were also the clubs that would have the most impact on her future.

When Brittany started cross country, she had never run anything longer than short sprints. She was not prepared for the physical strength and will that are involved in a cross country race. In fact, her first race in the sixth grade was a disaster. She finished the 1½ mile race but was doubled over with exhaustion and was almost dead last. She never placed that season, but she never quit either.

Brittany and her middle school cross country team.

Aside from being a determined person, Brittany was motivated to help her team win. In cross country, the first five runners for each team receive points based on the position they place. Having the team do well was the most important thing to Brittany. So a year later, during her seventh-grade season, she set two goals—to place high enough to help her team and to win at least one ribbon. When you place in the top ten you win a ribbon. Those ribbons were important to Brittany. Most kids her age already had ribbons and trophies from various sports but, despite enjoying sports so much, Brittany had never won any. It should come as no surprise that she now was able to accomplish this easily. She began to improve as a runner and started to close the gap between her and the competition. She had a good season and managed to win many ribbons but never placed better than seventh.

By eighth grade, Brittany won several second-place ribbons but first place still eluded her. It did not, however, elude the Seabury team. They took first place in the league and Brittany got a taste of that success. She was developing a real appreciation for long distance running, but her heart was definitely on the track . . . or, in Brittany's case, on the soccer field.

That's because Seabury Hall does not actually have a track. They paint white lines on a soccer field for makeshift lanes and finish lines. The conditions, though, didn't discourage Brittany. She loved running there. She enjoyed sprinting across the field as horses from the nearby stable grazed by the fence to watch. Running in nature was the greatest thrill in the world to Brittany, as it combined her two great loves: running and the outdoors.

Although her events were the fifty and the hundred-meter dash, and the hurdles, she made sure to watch every event. Brittany was a natural team leader, always enthusiastic and encouraging. Yes, she wanted to win herself, but she was happy just being out there rooting for her teammates. After going through what she had gone through, running and having fun was enough. Winning was the icing on the cake.

By the end of eighth grade, Brittany's injury was officially behind her. When her plane landed back on Maui after her final checkup at The Shriners Hospital for Children in Oahu, she realized that she had turned a page in her life. After seven long years of rehab, treatment, and checkups, it was finally over. Truthfully, Brittany had mixed emotions. She had been flying over to Oahu regularly since the second grade; it was like her second home. Yes, she was thrilled to be considered healed, but she would dearly miss the friends she'd made there.

For the rest of her life, these memories were a source of inspiration, a constant reminder that she was lucky to be alive. Now, thoughts of those less fortunate still drive her to continue running when everything in her body is telling her to stop.

Totally exhausted after a run.

Chapter Five

Pies, Pies, Pies

The 2003 cross country season was Brittany's introduction to high school running. During this season, she went through some amazing physical changes. One was a growth spurt, which made her stronger, faster, and able to run longer distances without tiring. These changes seemed to take place overnight. When she hit the trails her freshman year, she knew right away that something had clicked for her.

That freshman season was highlighted by the return of Tia Ferguson. Tia had moved to the mainland a year earlier, but was returning to Seabury Hall for her senior year. She was a state champion in several events and inspired Brittany with her dedication to running. Tia was a great motivator for the team as well, but especially for Brittany.

In chasing Tia throughout the season, Brittany improved drastically. In fact, she ran well enough to qualify for the state meet.

Although she did not place in the meet, she did do well enough to make the Maui Interscholastic League (MIL) All-Stars. This honor is awarded to the top ten runners in Maui. Brittany, of course, was quite proud of this accomplishment. As one of two freshmen on the team, she learned first hand from the more experienced runners about the dedication it took to succeed in cross country.

That spring, Brittany had her first real introduction to track under the direction of the Seabury track coach, Rudy Huber. Before high school, Brittany had been running to have fun, nothing more. During the fall cross country season, when Brittany had raced in Tia's shadow, she'd learned a great deal about being a competitor and she was ready to apply that to the track. Coach Rudy noticed Brittany's great potential and decided to have her run the four hundred meter dash in the first meet of the season. Brittany had never run this race before. In fact, she had never run on a track before—only on the grass of the soccer field or on trails during cross country.

When she lined up next to the other runners, the hard ground beneath her feet felt strange. She had no idea how fast or slow she would be on this new surface. Her feet gripped the ground below her and she took a long, deep breath. When the gun sounded, signaling the runners to go, Brittany took off like a rocket. After just a few strides, she was well out ahead of the pack. In just those first few steps, it was clear that Brittany was a serious competitor. She ran the race in 63 seconds, which qualified her for the state meet—after her first race ever on a track!

More important, this race cemented in Brittany's mind that she was going to be a runner. Until then, Brittany had raced with little or no training. She was now realizing that the best runners worked hard to be competitive. From this point forward, she no longer ran simply because she could—now she was running to win. She made that very clear during the MIL finals at the Yamamoto Track & Field Facility. Brittany ran the four hundred meter dash in 59.02 seconds, winning the race and shattering a twenty-four-year record. Her record setting time still holds today!

Once Brittany started winning races, she didn't stop.

During her freshman track season, Brittany ran the one hundred meter, the two hundred, the four hundred, the eight hundred, the fifteen hundred, the three thousand, and even did the long jump. She did well in all of them. She placed fourth in the state meet in the four hundred meter dash and, even though she was only fourteen, people in the Maui track world were already starting to talk about her.

Coach Rudy summed up Brittany's potential when he was interviewed about her in the Maui News: "Brittany has that drive, she's a special athlete," Huber said. "She's probably the most versatile runner in the state. She's the only runner I know who can run a 13.1 in the hundred and go all the way up to the three thousand."

Despite her success on the track, Brittany stayed involved in other sports. She was unwilling to focus solely on one activity. That just wasn't her style. The High School sports program was set up in trimesters, so Brittany played soccer during the second trimester, between cross country and track. She thought it would be a fun team sport, as well as a good way to stay in shape.

As the fastest player on the soccer field, her main assignment was to stick with the best player on the opposing team. Brittany did it well. What she was lacking in soccer skills, she made up for with determination and speed. This enabled her to play at the varsity level during her freshman year.

Aside from sports, Brittany spent much of her time in ninth grade babysitting and baking pies—lots and lots of pies. As a young girl recovering from serious burns and forced to stay inside a lot, Brittany had taught herself how to bake. The Young family had fruit trees on their property which Brittany used for her pies. She especially loved the apples and the white peaches.

Being an amazing baker came in handy during the end of her freshman year. Brittany's Spanish teacher was planning to take a group of students on a tour of Spain that summer. It sounded very exciting and Brittany wanted to go more than anything else she could think of. She pleaded her case to her mother. Mrs. Young realized that Brittany was serious but knew they couldn't afford the trip.

Although she never thought Brittany would be able to do it in such a short time, Mrs. Young told her: "If you can raise the money, you can go."

Brittany never backed down from a challenge. She estimated that she would need about $3,000 to go on the trip. Although she only had a few months to raise the money, she pursued her goal aggressively. She started by babysitting every chance she got. But after a month or so, she realized that she wouldn't be able to make enough money that way. For the next week, she laid awake in bed at night, wondering what to do.

The answer came to her as she stood in her kitchen, pulling a hot apple pie from the oven. "Mom, do you think anyone would buy my pies if I sold them?"

Mrs. Young loved her daughter's pies, and was sure that they would sell. But to make $3,000, Brittany would have to sell an impossible number of pies. "I'm sure they would," she answered. "I don't know if you'd be able to. . ."

"I think I can," Brittany said, before her mother could finish her sentence.

Within months, family and friends all over Kula and Makawao Town were enjoying Brittany's homemade peach, apple, pumpkin, mango, and original Japanese fruit pies. After school, she was baking three or four pies every night! A few months later, Brittany sold her final pie, after raising $4,000 for her trip—$1,000 more than she needed!

Unfortunately, Spain never happened. Shortly before they were supposed to leave, there was a terrorist bombing in Morocco, which is really close to Spain. With the events of September 11, 2001 still looming in their minds, Brittany's parents decided it wasn't safe for Brittany to travel abroad. Regretfully, she put her "pie" money into the bank and hoped for another trip in the future.

She didn't have to wait long. At the end of her freshman year, Coach Rudy decided to take some runners to Baltimore, Maryland to race against some of the best runners on the east coast. Brittany was ecstatic. She had never been to Maryland and was excited to compete. Maui is a small island, so Brittany knew most of her competitors, as well as their running styles. To visit someplace new, and face new runners, would be a great challenge.

Brittany and her friend Erin at the Capitol Building in Washington DC.

When they first arrived in Washington DC, which is only about thirty minutes from Baltimore, the girls took some time to sightsee. They only had one day to see the city, and although it rained, it didn't slow them down. In a lightning fast tour, they saw the Washington Monument, the White House, the Lincoln Memorial, the Jefferson Memorial, the United States Holocaust Memorial Museum, and as much of the Smithsonian as they could.

Brittany, who loved taking hikes in the beautiful surroundings of Maui, didn't realize how much she would enjoy her "city hike." It was like nothing she had ever experienced. At the same time, the feelings that coursed through her body as she looked at the historic buildings were similar to those she felt while viewing unique flowers and rushing waterfalls back home. Wherever she was, Brittany was enthralled by the world around her, and really took the time to appreciate it.

Washington DC was a far cry from her small island, but she couldn't get enough of it. Brittany was excited to share the experience with her friends and family. She couldn't wait to tell them that she had sat by the wrought iron fence in front of the White House! Brittany and her friend, Erin, still laugh about the aggressive "spy" squirrels that were bugging them there—one actually bit her butt as she sat on the wall.

One of the "spy" squirrels at the White House.

These great experiences almost made her forget why she had come to Maryland in the first place: to run. The next day came quickly. When the girls arrived at the track, they were intimidated by the expensive running shoes, sleek windbreakers, and sponsorship tents that were a part of this "big time" track event. Not to mention the incredibly large leg muscles on some of the runners!

As most of her teammates whispered to one another nervously, Brittany tried to stay focused. Still, she was anxious about how she would fare against these talented runners. It was one thing to be the best on Maui, but Brittany knew that her times needed to be faster if she was going to compete nationally.

Running the four hundred meter race first, Brittany was shocked by the speed of the other girls. She didn't even make it to the finals. In Maui, even as a fourteen-year-old freshman, she had always made the finals. Although she was disappointed, she managed to put it behind her by the time the eight hundred came around. She had planned to run her regular race strategy: *stay behind the leaders until the last two hundred meters, then start your kick, and out-sprint them to the finish line.*

That is not how things went. Brittany started out just behind the leaders, as she had planned. But when she was about to make her move, she found herself trapped in a tight pack. She couldn't cut the corner, and ended up smashed in the middle of about fifteen girls. The pace was fast, but Brittany knew that she could run faster—if only she could break out. She had never raced in such a large group and found herself getting bumped and jostled around by older, stronger, and more experienced runners.

With the race more than half over, Brittany tried to force her body forward on the inside. Just as she passed a few girls, she was nudged into the metal edge that bordered the infield. She stumbled onto the track and barely managed to get back up and finish the race.

Overall, it was a disappointing day, but it did provide a valuable lesson. The runners in Maui were often passive. The bumping and jostling style of these East Coast runners was something Brittany would have to deal with if she was going to run in bigger meets. And Brittany definitely planned to do that.

When she boarded the flight back to Maui, she knew that she'd be back. This was only the beginning.

Back home in Maui, Brittany sits on the track bleachers and reflects on her race in DC.

Chapter Six

Too Much

It had become obvious at the meet in Maryland that Brittany needed some work to win on a national level. When her sophomore year began, Tia was starting college on the mainland. This meant that there were no runners on Brittany's team that could really push her. That's why it was suggested that she train with a different team: the boy's team.

The top runners on the Seabury boy's cross country team ended up being Brittany's training partners. Although hanging out with boys all the time wasn't quite as fun as hanging out with the girls, Brittany welcomed the challenge of running with them. She loved to train—the harder, the better.

Cross country training usually consists of daily twenty to sixty-minute runs, as well as weightlifting three times a week. But Brittany wanted more. In addition to practices, she would get up at five thirty in the morning to run before school. She loved her quiet morning runs, enjoying the sights and sounds of a rural town waking up with the rising sun.

The extra training paid off. Brittany had an excellent sophomore season. She ran extremely strong and took first place in almost all of her races. She ended the season as the Maui Interscholastic League champion, which was rare for a sophomore. She was also, once again, on her way to the state meet which was being held on the Big Island. Brittany enjoyed traveling. It brought back memories of being a little girl and flying with her mother to get her legs checked. Although for some, these memories would be something that they would want to leave behind, Brittany cherished them. Her injury was a constant reminder of her strength and what she'd overcome.

Sophomore year: Brittany and her cross country teammates.

At the state cross country meet, Brittany started out the race running alongside the other Maui runners. But soon, the need to sprint took over and she started to pull away. She was in a zone, and had no idea how many girls she had passed. There were more than 185 runners, so it was hard to tell. When she crossed the finish line, she was excited because she thought she had placed around tenth. She wouldn't find out for sure until the awards ceremony.

Brittany was confused as she listened to the names being announced for the top twenty runners. *Why aren't they calling my name?* she wondered. Just as this thought entered her mind, the announcer said, "In fourth place, from Seabury Hall…"

Brittany never actually heard the announcer say her name because the shrieks from her teammates drowned out the loudspeaker. Brittany was ecstatic. She had hoped to do well, but a fourth place out of 185 of the best runners in the state was far better than she had expected. It was certainly a far cry from last ear, when she was ninety-seventh!

Her success in this race made Brittany think differently about running. She had been running both cross country and track for years, but she had always preferred track. With this recent success, she was discovering that she might have an equal passion for cross country and track.

When cross country ended, Coach Rudy advised against Brittany playing soccer, as she had done in years past. His concern was the major injury risk involved with this sport, but he did recommend paddling as a way for Brittany to develop her upper body strength. Paddling is a big sport in Hawaii. It requires strength and stamina, as well as a fierce determination to outrace both the competitors and nature. The ocean can be unforgiving at times and there are many days when the paddlers must endure dangerous conditions. But that was just what Brittany wanted—an adventure. When she heard from some of the team members how difficult the sport could be, she signed up right away.

During her first season, Brittany was moved up to the varsity team and given the position of stroker. There are six girls in the outrigger canoe: one steersman and five paddlers. The paddler in the front is called the stroker because he or she sets the pace for the boat. The stroker must be someone who won't give up, even when it seems that pulling one more stroke is impossible. Predictably, that person was Brittany. She had strength and stamina and was used to pushing through pain. Plus, she never gave up.

Brittany and the Seabury paddling team.

The team trained at the Kahului Harbor on the North Shore. Although the water didn't sparkle there like the resort beaches people swam in, it was still beautiful. Being on the water with friends, feeling the salt air on her skin, and physically pushing her body to the limit was awesome. Brittany also loved the competition. She found the regattas (races) fun, but also extremely challenging.

High school regattas are a half mile long. There are usually about six canoes, widely spaced, positioned next to their colored flag. When the starter, who is up ahead in a motor boat, gives the final command, the teams take off. They race a quarter mile out, go around their corresponding colored flag, and race a quarter mile back to their starting position.

The Seabury team had a great season and qualified for the state meet in Waikiki on Oahu. Brittany loved being with her teammates and was excited to go, but she also had a problem—the state regatta was the same day as her first track meet of the season! Because the two events were on different islands, there was no way she could do both. Brittany talked with her coaches and it was decided that she would go to the regatta on Oahu. Then, on her return, she would jump into the track season. Both coaches agreed on this course of action, but Coach Rudy was concerned about Brittany wearing herself out. It just seemed like too much.

She started the track season a week late, with no break period for her body to recover from the regatta. On any given day she would do as many as twelve four-hundred meter runs with minimal rest in between. She also did weight training three times each week.

Her training paid off at the MIL time trials in April, where she won the four hundred meter dash in 59:12 seconds. Although this time was just shy of breaking the record of 59.02, which she had set, it was fast enough to make her the number one seed for the MIL Championship meet.

She ran well in the four hundred meter dash two days later, but lost the MIL Championship in a photo finish to her good friend Erin Wooldridge from King Kekaulike High School. They had competed against each other for years and their races were always close. Although they were tough competitors from rival schools, it was common to see them hugging and joking before the start of a race. Brittany was happy for Erin, even though she was disappointed about losing this race.

Erin and Brittany share a hug shortly after competing against one another.

There was a silver lining, however. Brittany bounced right back to win first place in the eight hundred meter dash. So, for the third time this year, Brittany was on her way to a state championship.

With the state meet around the corner, Brittany could feel her demanding schedule beginning to wear her down. She was always tired—falling asleep the moment her head hit the pillow and barely able to wake up in the morning. Going to school, fulfilling her committee obligations, running every afternoon (and often in the morning as well), then studying until late into the night was simply too much. Plus, Brittany was also involved in a community service project called Dancing Palette. This worthwhile program took up two hours every Sunday, her only day off.

Dancing Palette, started by a girl at Seabury Hall whose brother was handicapped, helps young children with disabilities. Brittany's memories of the children she'd met at The Shriners Hospital for Children, as well as memories of her own time in a wheelchair, made it easy for her to relate. Brittany's role in Dancing Palette was to organize activities such as crafts, baking, music programs, and games. She was also responsible for fundraising, to ensure that the program would not only continue, but grow enough to help even more children.

The hectic schedule, however, finally caught up with her. Brittany had never really recovered from paddling season two months earlier. By the time the state track meet came around in April, she didn't feel her best—and it showed. She was unnaturally winded and felt weak. Despite her fatigue, she managed to place a respectable fifth in the four hundred meter dash, although she took a disappointing eighth place in the eight hundred.

Even though she was disappointed with the results of the state meet, the running world still recognized her incredible talent. In cross country, Brittany was voted the Maui Interscholastic League Female Runner of the Year. In track, she made the All-Star Team (top runner in each running event at the MIL Finals) for the eight hundred meter run and Honorable Mention for the four hundred (though she still held the MIL record). She was also named the

Seabury Hall Female Athlete of the Year, an award usually reserved for seniors.

These accolades were wonderful, but Brittany was ignoring the signals her body was giving her. She needed a break.

Brittany trains on the track at King Keaulike High School.

Chapter Seven

No More Changes!

The summer before her junior year of high school, Brittany once again trained with the summer track club to prepare for the fall season. She had run last summer and it had been especially fun because Jake and Makenna had run with her. They were not running this summer, but Brittany hung out with her family all the time anyhow.

Still, the track club was fun because Brittany's friend Erin was running, as well as her other good friend—another Brittany— Brittany Feiteira. These three girls were known as The Three Compadres. They were inseparable, on and off the track.

Brittany's summer was going wonderfully until the day that her father made a shocking announcement: "We sold the house." As the words left his lips, there was stunned silence in the room. Although everybody knew the day was coming, it still didn't seem real. Over the years, Mr. and Mrs. Young had put the house up for sale many times, only to take it off the market again. They went back and forth, not sure whether they wanted to sell it. In the meantime, Brittany had become very attached to her home. She secretly hoped it would never sell.

Brittany had lived there since she was two weeks old and had spent most of her childhood exploring every square inch of the wooded property. And then there was Jackie, Brittany's neighbor and playmate since the day she'd moved there. Jackie was like one of the family and it just didn't seem right to move and leave her behind, even though their new home was only one town away.

As Brittany sat on the floor of her bedroom, boxing up everything that belonged to her, she thought about all the wonderful memories she had of her home. She thought of all the time she had spent sitting on the window seat in her bedroom, enjoying the sweet smell of the eucalyptus trees. And lying in her bed at night, watching the moon glide silently across the sky as she ran tomorrow's race over and over in her head.

There were also memories that, although painful, were a big part of her. The road. . . the protea farm. . . the burn pit. . . the run home. . . . Brittany recalled it all as if it had been yesterday. She had no desire whatsoever to leave any of it behind. It was a big part of her life—among other things, there were seven years of recovery associated with that house. In the end, Brittany had no choice. The house was sold. She sadly finished taping up the boxes and glanced out the window for the last time.

Shortly after moving, Brittany and five other girls went with Coach Rudy to the Pacific Association Junior Olympic Track and Field Championships in California. Brittany was excited for the distraction. She always enjoyed running out of state. Plus, her friend Erin was one of the girls going.

The five girls had a blast, but they also made an impressive showing on the track. Brittany took first place in the eight hundred meter dash and set a personal record of 2:17 minutes. She also took second place in the fifteen hundred with a personal record of 4:57 minutes, and fourth place in the four hundred with a time of 59.51 seconds. In addition, the girls teamed up to run the 4x400 meter relay, and sprinted their way into an impressive second place. Her success in California was a great way to bounce back from the previous season's disappointing finish.

When she returned to school in the fall, Brittany found out that Coach Rudy was no longer at Seabury Hall. This was a major disappointment as Brittany began her critical junior season. The junior year is the most important year for an athlete in search of a college scholarship. It is during this year that most colleges begin looking closely at the athletes they plan on offering scholarships to in the fall. Brittany knew this, which made her twice as nervous about Coach Rudy's disappearing act.

Between that, moving out of the house she'd grown up in, and her demanding schedule, Brittany was stressed. Life was changing and this weighed heavily on her as the cross country season started.

Luckily, her new coach, Tom Rehrer was a familiar face. Tom had coached the Seabury boy's cross country team as well as the distance runners on the Seabury track teams for several years. This was great, because Brittany knew him well. Still, it would be a big adjustment.

Brittany with her new coach, Tom Rehrer.

Although she went into her junior season with a good attitude, it was tough on her. Despite her winning races, Brittany's body was continuing to wear down—big time. In fact, she was having trouble breathing at times. At first she tried to brush it off. She even trained harder to compensate for her lack of energy. This strategy worked for a while, but only a short while.

Once again, Brittany qualified for the state cross country meet. She was also named the MIL Runner of the Year, again. But her health was getting worse and worse. After unsuccessfully trying to run through it, Brittany finally sought medical attention. She was told that she might have exercise-induced asthma. This is a breathing disorder that develops when one is under intense physical stress, such as running. Because of this, Brittany was given an inhaler she was supposed to use before she ran. Although the inhaler helped, she still didn't have her full strength back.

When she got to the cross country state meet in the fall of 2005, Brittany was determined to focus on the race, not her breathing. She got so caught up in all the pre-race excitement, though, that she forgot to use her inhaler before she ran.

Brittany started the race strong, but with only a half mile behind her, she could tell that something was wrong. Her breathing was labored and her lungs felt like they were going to explode. This made Brittany angry. It had been nine years since her accident, and her legs were great . . . and now this!

For the first time in her life, she didn't know if she would be able to finish the race. But Brittany was a fighter, not a quitter, so she struggled through the three miles and finished in fifty-fifth place, a very disappointing end to her cross country season. Despite that, the Seabury team did well and Brittany was enthusiastic about their results, if not her own.

When the team returned to Maui, a reporter for the school yearbook asked her what her proudest moment of the cross country season was, expecting her to talk about one of her many great races. But Brittany, without hesitating, answered, "Definitely the state meet. I ran the worst race of my life, but I finished, and all my girls ran their best races, and fastest times all season. I was super stoked for them."

Brittany's love for her teammates is mutual. In fact, her cross country team voted Brittany the captain during her junior season. She was the track captain the year before as well, and had been a co-captain for cross country as well.

When the track season started in the spring, Brittany, in her usual leadership role, had everybody psyched for a good season. With a new coach in charge of the track team, there were certainly going to be some changes, but Brittany felt good about them.

Tom Rehrer is primarily a long distance coach. That fact, combined with Brittany's success on the mainland in the eight hundred meter, was the reason they decided to have Brittany concentrate on longer races. Coach Tom was confident that Brittany could win the state meet in the eight hundred if they paced her and didn't let her burn herself out. Being a state champion was a lofty goal, but Brittany thought that she could accomplish it with the right training and race strategy.

Coach Tom was also working hard to help Brittany relax and not feel so pressured. Brittany expected more from herself than anybody else and sometimes that worked against her. His approach was different than Coach Rudy's, but it seemed to be exactly what Brittany needed. Coach Tom wasn't convinced that Brittany had exercise induced asthma, either. His thought was that she had simply over trained. Her incredible drive to succeed had actually backfired. In keeping up with her many activities, and training year round twice as hard as everyone else, she had actually worn herself down. This season, Coach Tom made sure Brittany was more careful with her schedule, and took some time to relax her body and mind.

Brittany spends a lot of her free time hiking or hanging out by the water. These activities help to relax her body and mind.

Brittany still practiced hard, but she enjoyed it even more now under the direction of Coach Tom. Because Seabury Hall does not have a track, you often find the team practicing at the King Kekaulike High School track, just down the road. Like Seabury, it sits high on the side of Haleakala and has a commanding view of the Pacific Ocean. It is a common sight to see Brittany, ponytail flying behind her, sprinting around the track long after the others have gone in. Her beautiful running form is highlighted by her long, powerful strides—she is something to watch, even from a distance.

Brittany used those assets as she moved to an easy win during the first track meet of the spring season. Brittany ran a 2:19 for the eight hundred meter run and felt strong doing it. She had no trouble breathing and was confident that she'd finally cleared that hurdle.

After that race, Brittany and her coach decided that this season she would run only the eight hundred, the fifteen hundred, and the three thousand meter runs in each meet, with an occasional four hundred if her schedule called for a sprint workout (she ran the four hundred in the MIL trials and won it). Brittany wanted to run the shorter races and the relays like she used to do, but her training was now geared to focus only on the longer events. This new program worked so well that she raced through that entire season without losing a single race!

When the state track meet came up on May 13, 2006, Brittany, with the help of Coach Tom, was ready. It was her junior season, the state meet, and her biggest chance to shine. College scouts all over Hawaii and the mainland would be interested in the outcome of this race.

Brittany wore a focused expression on the starting line—

she was trying to be the best eight hundred meter runner in the state of Hawaii. Seeded number one, she was on the rail.

"Runners, take your mark!" The eight elite runners shifted into their favorite starting stances. They would stay in their lanes for a hundred meters, then cut to the post.

"Get set!" There was an audible intake of breaths as the girls tried to calm the butterflies that were wreaking havoc on their insides.

"BANG!" The starting gun exploded as the biggest race of Brittany's life began.

Chapter Eight

Born to Run

The runners took off. For the most part, they were all still together as they hit the hundred-meter mark. As usual, Brittany's strategy was to run in second, on the shoulder of the lead runner, until about the last two hundred meters. At that point, she would shift into another gear—one that she and Coach Tom felt no other runner in the race could match. They had researched all the runners and felt confident about their strategy.

After the first hundred, Brittany could hear her teammates cheering from the stands. "Go Brittany!" She knew they were right, she had to *go*. She was bunched in with the other runners, slightly behind the leader. Not wanting to let the lead runner, a strong runner from Punahou High School get away, Brittany, at the two hundred mark, moved out into lane four to get around the pack. This added a little distance to the run, but Brittany knew it was the only way to get up front.

She passed everyone but the lead runner, and settled into her stride, as planned. The two girls started to pull away from the group and were significantly ahead at the four hundred meter mark.

"Sixty-seven!" The official called out the split time for the first lap. Brittany was three seconds off the pace she wanted, the split time she needed to make her goal of running a 2:15 or less. She had run consecutive sixty-four second laps at practice, so knew she had it in her. But, though she was behind her pace, she knew that these were the best runners in the state and if she accelerated too soon, she might be out-sprinted in the end. Reaching her goal would be nice, but her first priority was to win the race. She held back and stuck to her plan.

Brittany planned to start her sprint when she hit the last two hundred meters, but her adrenaline kicked in early. With three hundred meters to go, Brittany started sprinting. That was a little early to start the kick. The question now was: could she keep it up to the finish line? The Punahou runner did not keep pace, letting the two runners who had previously been in third and fourth quickly pass her. They began to close the gap. She could hear their feet pounding behind her and knew that her only chance at victory was to maintain the sprint all the way to the finish line.

They headed into the final curve. The fans were on their feet as Brittany sprinted for the line. The screaming from the stands made her think that the other runners were right on her heels, so she pushed even harder.

In the end, Brittany crossed the finish line a full second ahead of the second-place finisher. She was the new state champion in the eight hundred meter run!

Brittany was thrilled, but her time of 2:19:08, although fast, was not as fast as she had hoped. Both Coach Tom, and Brittany, believe that Brittany can significantly reduce her eight hundred time to compete nationally. With few runners of her caliber in Hawaii, Brittany will have to find the drive from within to push herself to the next level. Brittany has already set high running goals for her senior year, with the dream of running competitively in college.

The biggest obstacle that Brittany faces in realizing that dream is her love of doing everything. Coach Tom knows that Brittany has not yet reached her full potential in running. He knows that a big reason that she was able to win the state meet was because she focused on one event. He is constantly telling Brittany that she needs to prioritize—and not be involved in so many different things. He believes that if she focuses on running, with the eight hundred meter run at the forefront of her training, her potential is limitless.

Right now, though, she's having too much fun to be so serious.

In an interview that focused on Brittany, Coach Tom said, "Brittany likes a lot of things: art, all different sports, social activities, and she's got a lot of friends—she's a typical sixteen-year-old girl. But at some level I think she's probably fighting with herself, kind of asking, 'Do I want to give up some of this stuff to pursue it for real?'"

Coach Tom believes that Brittany will be an impressive college runner. In addition to her talent, Brittany has another very important quality for a runner—the heart of a champion.

Brittany may not be quite ready to prioritize her interests yet, but she is definitely motivated, in all areas of her life. Her fellow students voted her as their student body president for her senior year. Knowing Brittany, it will be another active year for this talented girl. Brittany has no plans of slowing down. She dreams big and has set huge goals for her last year of high school, both on and off the track. Brittany also has a big dream for the future—to organize a 10 K run to support The Shriners Hospitals for Children. Brittany is very appreciative of the care she received there and she would like to give something back.

In May, 2006, as a requirement for a speech class, Brittany had to deliver a speech in front of her entire high school. The speech was to be about a life-altering experience. Brittany once again risked ridicule as she stood at the podium, ready to tell the story of that fateful day. The pounding of her heart drowned out the rain that beat down on the metal roof. Four hundred pairs of eyes were focused on her, waiting for her to tell a story—a story that few had heard.

Brittany knew that she had a reputation in school. She was certainly known for her athletic talent and probably her bubbly personality, too. Yet some students misunderstood her. They thought she was obsessive about her workouts and perhaps a little too enthusiastic about life in general. Today she would explain to them why.

Brittany took a deep breath and pushed her memory of the third grader who thought her legs were "gross" from her mind. She knew that in speaking about her accident, she was risking ridicule again. Things were different this time, though. The scars were still there, but they were not gross to Brittany. She had grown to see them in a positive light, a reminder that she was lucky to be standing at this podium—lucky to be standing at all.

Brittany looked out at the crowd and confidently retold her inspiring story. She told of the burn pit, her run up the hill on Cooke Road, her scarred feet, her fears, and her seven-year recovery. She talked about the sick and burned children she had come to know, and how they affected her life. She talked about the life lessons she had learned. She described her experience at Shriners Hospitals, not in terms of her own pain and problems, but with sympathy for the other children there, and how they changed her outlook on life.

"Along my journey to healing I was exposed to so many other children, older and younger, with medical problems far worse than my own. Once you think you have a 'bad' situation you need to step out and realize how lucky you really are. There is always, and I can guarantee always, someone else out there with far worse of a 'bad' situation."

Everyone was visibly moved as she described the details of her physical and emotional journey. Brittany ended her speech with a famous quote, answering the most often asked question: Why do you run?

"John F. Kennedy once said, 'As we express our gratitude, we must never forget that the highest appreciation is not to utter words, but to live by them.' I not only learned the typical lesson, 'don't take every moment—or should I say, *step* you take for granted.' But I also realized that you must always take action upon what you say you learn. For the past several years I have often been questioned as to why I run. Now you know. It is not genetics, it's determination. Determination to show how appreciative I am that I was given the ability to heal. Running is not a pain, it's a privilege. Every step I take when I walk, every stride I take when I run, I embrace what I have because I never know when all that I have could be gone."

Brittany still bears physical scars on her feet, but she is thankful for every step she takes as she confidently strides into the future. Nothing can diminish the sparkle in her eyes, the laughter in her voice, or the genuine love she has for life and for others. Brittany's heart is as big as her incredible talent. She was born to win races, born to inspire other people—but more than anything, she was born to run.